COPYRIGHT AND PERMISSIONS

WHAT EVERY WRITER AND EDITOR SHOULD KNOW

ELSA PETERSON

THE-EFA.ORG

Copyright © 2020, 2012, 2008, 1996 by Elsa Peterson
Cover and design © 2020 Editorial Freelancers Association
New York, NY

All rights reserved.
No part of this publication may be reproduced, distributed, or transmitted in any form or by any means, including, but not limited to, photocopying, recording, or other electronic or mechanical methods, without the prior written permission of the publisher, except in the case of brief quotations embodied in critical reviews and certain other noncommercial uses permitted by copyright law. For permission requests, write to the publisher at "Attention: Publications Chairperson," at the address below.

266 West 37th St. 20th Floor
New York, NY 10018
office@the-efa.org

ISBN paperback   978-1-880407-37-0
ISBN ebook   978-1-880407-38-7

Published in the United States of America by the Editorial Freelancers Association.
Subject Categories: **LANGUAGE ARTS & DISCIPLINES** | Writing | Business Aspects | Publishers & Publishing Industry | LAW | Intellectual Property | Copyright | **BUSINESS & ECONOMICS** | Industries | Media & Communications

Legal Disclaimer
While the publisher and author have made every attempt to verify that the information provided in this book is correct and up to date, the publisher and author assume no responsibility for any error, inaccuracy, or omission.

The advice, examples, and strategies contained herein are not suitable for every situation. Neither the publisher nor author shall be liable for damages arising therefrom. This book is not intended for use as a source of legal or financial advice. Running a business involves complex legal and financial issues. You should always retain competent legal and financial professionals to provide guidance.

EFA Publications Director: Robin Martin
Copyeditor: Brooke Smith
Proofreader: Joy Drohan
Indexer: Elliot Linzer
Book Designer: Kevin Callahan | BNGO Books
Cover Designer: Ann Marie Manca

The author of this work is not an attorney, and this book is not to be taken as legal advice. It is meant solely to offer information to editorial freelancers and others in publishing. If you have questions about the legality of a particular use of copyright material, consult a lawyer.

ACKNOWLEDGMENTS

The author gratefully acknowledges the contributions of the EFA editing and production team; of the students in her Greenwich Continuing Education and EFA copyright classes; and of the late Ronald L. Freed, who as President of European American Music Distributors Corporation was the best boss a young professional could wish for.

Contents

ACKNOWLEDGMENTS	iii
PART I: INTRODUCTION TO COPYRIGHT	1
What Is Copyright?	2
Copyright Facts and Fallacies	4
How Is Copyright Established?	7
What Cannot Be Copyrighted?	11
Public Domain and Fair Use	12
Patent, Trademark, Privacy, and Libel	15
How Long Does Copyright Protection Last?	16
PART II: COPYRIGHT IN THE TWENTY-FIRST CENTURY	19
The Digital Millennium Copyright Act	20
Social Media	20
Digital Collaboration	23
Google Books and the Internet Archive	25
Is Copyright Obsolete?	27
Will the Duration of Copyright Be Extended?	30
PART III: GUIDE TO PERMISSIONS EDITING	33
What Is Permissions Editing?	33
Four Basic Steps in Permissions Editing	35
Negotiating Fees	44
Dead Ends, Denials, and Disclaimers	46
Tips for Finding Permissions Editing Jobs	48

References	51
APPENDIX A: SAMPLE ACKNOWLEDGMENTS	53
APPENDIX B: SAMPLE PERMISSION REQUEST LETTER	55
APPENDIX C: RECOMMENDED RESOURCES	57
INDEX	59
About the Author	63
About the Editorial Freelancers Association (EFA)	64

PART I:

INTRODUCTION TO COPYRIGHT

This book is written by an editorial freelancer for the benefit of other editorial freelancers with the aim of covering the essentials of copyright as they relate to writers and editors. It is especially intended for those who work on a freelance basis because they can't rely on a corporate legal department to keep them out of trouble when it comes to copyright. I also hope this book will inform those who are interested in working as freelance permissions editors and those who may be in a position to hire permissions editors. As such, it offers information about how permissions editing is done in the publishing industry. It was written from the point of view of an American freelancer; it is hoped that readers who live and work in other countries may find it informative, but they will need to consult other sources to understand how copyright works in the country where they are based. While this book cannot provide legal advice, it offers knowledge about the law and its applications in the world of editorial freelancing.

Copyright is a vast, fascinating subject. Copyright can also be frustrating—especially when a writer wishes to use material that is protected by copyright and is told: "You can't use that without permission." The best way to avoid this kind of frustration is to be knowledgeable about copyright, and that means acquiring information that will enable the would-be user to know:

- whether the desired use of the material actually needs permission;
- if it does, where and how to seek permission; and
- what to do if permission is denied or is too expensive.

This is the kind of knowledge you will gain from this book.

This book is organized into three parts. Part I defines copyright and explains how it works. Part II discusses various aspects of the modern digital environment that have made copyright much more complex in the twenty-first century than it was in the days of ink on paper. The implications of the Digital Millennium Copyright Act are examined, as well as how social media and open-access initiatives such as Creative Commons may affect the entire concept of copyright.

Part III outlines the process of permissions editing, which can be a rewarding specialty for freelancers who have both the interest and the talent for the detective work it often involves. I will discuss how to negotiate fees with rights holders, and what to do if a permission cannot be secured. Part III concludes with a step-by-step guide offering advice on finding permissions editing jobs. In this part of the book, publishers are referred to as "clients" to avoid confusion with rights holders, since the latter are often also publishers.

The book concludes with appendixes offering examples of copyright acknowledgments, a sample permission request letter, and a list of resources that should be helpful for readers seeking more specialized commentary by legal experts.

With these broader ideas in mind, let's narrow our focus and examine what copyright is and how it works.

What Is Copyright?

In simplest terms, copyright is the right to copy. It is a body of law governing the right to reproduce and distribute a work; to display or perform it in public; and to create adaptations, translations, and other derivative works based upon it. Copyright is a form of intellectual property protection, a body of law designed to encourage creative endeavor by ensuring that original compositions and discoveries cannot be appropriated by unauthorized parties, but remain the property of their creators.

Copyright and Permissions

Copyright has been part of United States law ever since our nation was founded. Article I of the Constitution gives Congress the power "To promote the Progress of Science and useful Arts, by securing for limited Times to Authors and Inventors the exclusive Right to their respective Writings and Discoveries."

Writers, artists, musicians, filmmakers, and all other creators of material benefit from copyright because it gives them the exclusive right to use their creative output, and to license it to others if they so choose. Similarly, copyright benefits publishers by giving them legal recourse in cases of pirating and unauthorized copying. For the purposes of this book, *publisher* is defined as any business or entity that produces multiple copies of a tangible product containing copyrightable material; these products include print books and ebooks, magazines, videos, websites, blogs, and so forth.

In the United States, the Copyright Office of the Library of Congress is the central clearinghouse for copyrights and for information about how to make use of copyright. It offers a wealth of informative publications that can be downloaded free of charge from copyright.gov/. The publication that provides the essentials of copyright is a circular titled *Copyright Basics*, available in both English and Spanish at copyright.gov/circs/circ01.pdf. *Copyright Basics* lists the following broad categories of works as eligible for copyright protection:

- literary works
- musical works, including any accompanying words
- dramatic works, including any accompanying music
- pantomimes and choreographic works
- pictorial, graphic, and sculptural works
- motion pictures and other audiovisual works
- sound recordings
- architectural works

Copyright Basics goes on to explain that "these categories should be viewed quite broadly; for example, computer programs and most 'compilations' [are classified] as 'literary works'; maps and architectural plans [are classified] as 'pictorial, graphic, and sculptural works.'" For purposes of copyright, the material may exist on paper, on disk, on tape, on the internet, or in any other tangible medium.

Those who wish to read the full text of "Copyright Law of the United States and Related Laws Contained in Title 17 of the United States Code" can download it from the Copyright Office at copyright.gov/title17/.

Copyright Facts and Fallacies

Although copyright affects our lives in many subtle ways, the concept of copyright usually goes unrecognized by the general public. Even people who work with copyrighted material on a daily basis are often unaware of the ins and outs of how copyright works. Here are a few common beliefs about copyright; let's see how accurate they are.

> **Belief:** *Copyright can protect an idea or concept, such as the plot of a screenplay that has not yet been written.*

This is false. Copyright cannot protect an idea; it protects the tangible expression of an idea. As such, if the screenplay plot is jotted down in the notes app on a smartphone, or spoken into an audio recording device, or acted out in pantomime before a video recording device, then the jotting or the audio or video recording constitutes a tangible expression, and it can be copyrighted.

> **Belief:** *The word* copywritten *is the adjective corresponding to the noun copyright.*

This is incorrect. Copywriting is the act of writing copy, usually for advertising or marketing, and materials so written can be described as copywritten. That has nothing to do with their copyright status. When a work is protected by copyright, it is copyrighted.

> **Belief:** *A business can copyright certain words and slogans so that no one else can use them.*

This is not so. Copyright does not protect slogans or individual words. Words and slogans can be protected under trademark law, which is another form of intellectual property protection that operates differently from the way copyright does.

> **Belief:** *If a website has no encryption or other security protocols to prevent a user from downloading or copying and pasting that site's content, then the user can legally use that content without attribution, as if it were the user's own creation.*

This false belief can promote breaking the law. Regardless of how easy it is to obtain material found online, passing someone else's material off as one's own is plagiarism and can constitute copyright infringement. Some websites contain material that is free of copyright, or available for use without formal permission, but the burden is always on the user to determine whether material is protected and whether attribution to the source is required.

> **Belief:** *Copyright law allows the use of up to 10 percent of a work without permission; for example, one hundred words from a one-thousand-word article may be used without permission.*

This is a fallacy. The law's fair use provisions do allow small amounts of material to be used without permission, but the law does not specify any percentage or word count.

> **Belief:** *The creator of a work must display a copyright notice in a prominent place; otherwise the work is not protected.*

This is not true. Copyright law clearly states that copyright exists and belongs to the creator as soon as a work is fixed in tangible form.

> **Belief:** *If a work is in the public domain, meaning that it is not protected by copyright, someone can come along and copyright it so that no one else can use it.*

This misconception probably comes from the fact that someone can indeed copyright an adaptation, translation, arrangement, or other derivative work based on a work in the public domain. The underlying work itself, however, remains in the public domain and can be freely used.

> **Belief:** *If I use Twitter to send a really funny joke, or write a glowing review of a restaurant on TripAdvisor, or "like" a product on Facebook, the host sites (Twitter, TripAdvisor, or Facebook, as the case may be) own the copyright to my material. They can use it to promote their own site, or license it to someone else, such as the restaurant, for an ad. They can also collect it and publish it, for example, in a Best Twitter Jokes book.*

According to the Terms of Use on these and other sites, this is more or less true. The Terms of Use may give the user a few protections or privacy options, but most host sites like these claim ownership of the material users post. If you are concerned about losing control of your material on a given site, read the Terms before you post.

> **Belief:** *If I send my work to myself in a sealed envelope and don't open it, the postmark will prove that the work is mine, and this is an easier way to register my copyright than going through all the red tape of the Library of Congress.*

This does not work. There are several problems with this "do-it-yourself copyright" technique. First of all, the postmark only proves that the work existed at a certain time; it doesn't prove who created the work or when. Second, registration with the Library of Congress provides legal remedies that aren't provided by the sealed-envelope method. Third, the "red tape" of the Library of Congress really is not difficult to deal with, especially once you have read the information in this book.

We will examine some of these issues in greater depth in the following pages. I hope the foregoing examples will lead the reader to contemplate seriously some of the concerns surrounding copyright.

How Is Copyright Established?

As was mentioned above, copyright exists and belongs to the creator as soon as a work is fixed in tangible form. For example, if I write a poem on a cocktail napkin, that poem is instantly copyrighted and the copyright belongs to me. If I draw a sketch along with the poem, my drawing is copyrighted too, and the copyright also belongs to me. If I then take a photograph of the napkin, my photograph is copyrighted and the copyright belongs to me. If I create a video and my photograph of the napkin appears before the video camera, my video is copyrighted, and I don't need anyone's permission for the underlying work of the photograph of the napkin, because these are all my copyrights. Good for me!

But please also consider from the examples above how complicated permission would become if the poem, the drawing, the photograph, and the video were all created by different people.

Does copyright ever belong to someone other than the creator? Yes! If you browse through several books and examine the copyright page of each one, you will probably see that the book's copyright belongs to the publisher in many cases. This occurs because the creator of a work has transferred the copyright. It is not unusual for publishers to include clauses in their contracts transferring copyright from the author to the publisher. It should be noted that, instead of transferring copyright altogether, an author may assign copyright to the publisher for a limited period of time or for a limited number of editions of a book. An author may also retain copyright and grant a license—exclusive or, less commonly, nonexclusive—to a publisher to reproduce and distribute a book.

There are also circumstances where the creator of a work never owned the copyright in the first place. Under the Copyright Act of 1909, which was the main statute governing United States copyright until 1978, copyright was established through publication and affixing a copyright notice. Since publishers were generally the ones doing the publishing and printing the copyright notice in the front of the book, they were also, more often than not, the copyright holders under that law. The Copyright Act of 1976, which took effect in 1978, overturned that legal tradition, but it still provides for non-creators to own copyright in cases of corporate authorship and work made for hire. (Details of the work-for-hire concept are outlined in the Copyright Office circular *Works Made for Hire,* available at copyright.gov/circs/circ09.pdf.) When employees of a corporation (some journalists, for example) create copyrightable work in the course of their employment, the terms of their employment may specify that their employer owns copyright to the work they create. Companies also hire freelancers to create copyrightable work, requiring them to sign a Work for Hire Agreement that specifies that the work produced will belong to the company that hired the creator. Textbook publishers, for example, usually commission instructor manuals, student study guides, test banks, and other ancillaries on a work-for-hire basis. The author-for-hire may or may not receive credit on the cover, but the publisher typically retains all rights to the material created for hire.

Apart from these exceptions, the dominant situation today is for the creator of a work to own copyright from the moment the work is fixed in tangible form. Even though the creator doesn't have to do anything to enjoy copyright protection, there are two actions the creator can and should take to strengthen that protection: affixing a copyright notice to the work, and registering it with the Copyright Office of the Library of Congress. When a work bears a copyright notice and has been registered with the Copyright Office, the owner is in a much stronger position to take legal action in case the copyright is infringed upon or claimed by someone else. This is why many authors, artists, and other creators not only place a copyright notice on each of their works, but also file a Library of Congress copyright registration application before submitting the work to an agent or publisher for consideration.

A valid copyright notice is extremely simple to write. It consists of three elements: the word *copyright* or the symbol ©, the year of creation or first publication, and the name of the copyright owner. The notice should be affixed to every copy of the work in a clearly visible place, such as the first or last page of a piece of writing.

Copyright © 1993 by Sidney Harris, ScienceCartoonsPlus.com. Used by permission.

Registering a work with the Copyright Office involves more effort than writing a copyright notice, but it is no more difficult than, say, getting a driver's license or filling out a tax return. Although copyrights can be registered using paper forms available from the Copyright Office of the Library of Congress, electronic registration is strongly encouraged. It is done through the Registration Portal of the Copyright Office: copyright.gov/registration/.

Whether it is done on paper or electronically, copyright registration requires three things:

1. a copyright application;
2. an application fee of $45 or more (fee depends on the type of work, number of authors, and other factors); and
3. two copies of the work being registered, which can be uploaded online in some cases.

The Registration Portal begins with an instruction to log in on the Electronic Copyright Office (eCO) Registration System. Users who do not already have an account on the system are directed to create one. The system then guides the user through a menu that requires information such as the following.

1. **The work**: Specify the type of work being registered (literary, visual arts, etc.) and basic information about it such as whether it has been published, and the title and year of completion.
2. **Author**: Provide the name and contact information for the author or creator of the work.
3. **Copyright claimant**: This may be the same as in (2) above, or it may be the publisher or another party to whom the author has transferred copyright, or it may be the employer if the work is a work made for hire.
4. **Limitation of copyright claim**: This applies if the material being registered is based on some other work that has already been copyrighted.
5. **Rights and permissions contact**: This may be the same as the information in (2) above, or it may be the author's agent, lawyer, or some other person or firm authorized by the author to handle rights and permissions for the work being registered.
6. **Correspondence contact**: This may be the author, or it may be the author's agent, lawyer, or some other person or firm authorized to handle correspondence with the Copyright Office.
7. **Mail certificate to**: This is the mailing address where the author wants the Copyright Office to send the copyright certificate once the registration is completed.

8. **Deposit account number**: This applies only if the copyright claimant has placed funds on deposit with the Copyright Office to cover a substantial number of registrations; many publishers have deposit accounts for this purpose.

Circular 2, *Copyright Registration*, is available at copyright.gov/circs/. It provides a basic overview of the copyright registration process.

Among the benefits of copyright registration is the listing of the work in the Copyright Office's searchable online database. Accessible to the public at cocatalog.loc.gov/cgi-bin/Pwebrecon.cgi?DB=local&PAGE=, this database enables everyone to determine the copyright owner of every work that has been registered since 1978. Works published before January 1, 1978, are listed in the Library of Congress catalog, but this catalog is not digitized; it is accessible to the public during library opening hours in the Copyright Records Reading Room in Washington, DC.

A person registering a copyright might wonder, "If I want my work protected throughout the world, do I have to register it in any other country, or perhaps in *all* other countries?" In practical terms, the answer is no. Although there is no such thing as an international copyright that automatically protects a work throughout the world, the United States has agreements with many countries and groups of countries to honor one another's copyrights. The United States belongs to the Berne Convention and the Universal Copyright Convention, and has bilateral agreements with various individual countries that are not members of these larger conventions. In the judgment of the Copyright Office, a United States copyright registration is generally sufficient to protect a work throughout the world.

What Cannot Be Copyrighted?

As mentioned earlier in the list of common beliefs about copyright, copyright protects only works that have been fixed in tangible form. An idea for a screenplay is protected if it has been fixed in the form of a written plot summary, which could reside on a computer's hard drive and/or be printed on paper. It could also be fixed in the form of an audio recording of the writer's oral description of the plot. It cannot, however, be copyrighted if it only exists as an oral description that is neither transcribed nor recorded. Similarly, a musical composition is protected if it has been fixed in musical notation or in an audio or video recording, but it cannot be copyrighted if it only exists as a live performance in real time.

Beyond this "tangible form" provision, copyright law excludes certain other kinds of material. As the Copyright Office explains in the circular *Copyright Basics*, the following cannot be copyrighted, even if they exist in tangible form:

> - titles, names, short phrases, and slogans; familiar symbols or designs; mere variations of typographic ornamentation, lettering, or coloring; mere listings of ingredients or contents
> - ideas, procedures, methods, systems, processes, concepts, principles, discoveries, or devices, as distinguished from a description, explanation, or illustration
> - works consisting entirely of information that is common property and containing no original authorship [such as] standard calendars, height and weight charts, tape measures and rulers, and lists or tables taken from public documents or other common sources

Also ineligible for copyright protection are works by the United States government. The government takes the view that these works are paid for by taxpayers and may therefore be used, reproduced, and distributed freely. However, this does not always hold true for material created or published by state or local governments, public–private partnerships, or other government-related entities. For example, if you wished to reproduce a United States postage stamp, you might need to obtain multiple layers of permission. Similarly, speeches delivered by public officials are sometimes written by privately contracted writers.

Public Domain and Fair Use

Works that are not protected by copyright are in the public domain, meaning that they belong to the public and can be freely used, reproduced, adapted, translated, and so forth. No permission is needed and no attribution to any source is required. However, it is a fallacy that any published material was in the public domain because it is *accessible* to the public and not secret or proprietary information. By this logic, any newspaper, library book, or website would be in the public domain. This is *not* what "public domain" means when it comes to copyright law!

Public domain material includes not only the categories of works that the Copyright Office lists as being ineligible for copyright protection, but also works for which copyright was never established, and works whose copyright has expired.

People sometimes wonder why it can be legal to use material without permission even though that material is clearly protected by copyright. For example, why is it legal to quote excerpts from a newly published book in a book review? And why does this very book, which you are now reading, use quoted passages from some copyrighted sources? The answer is that this type of use falls under the fair use doctrine in copyright law. It is helpful to think of fair use as a way of reconciling the protections of copyright law with the free-speech provisions of the First Amendment. While the creators of writings, artwork, music, and so forth have the right to control their work and be compensated for it, citizens also have a right to free expression, which can sometimes include the use, within limits, of copyrighted material. Just what those limits are, however, is a question that is continually open to debate and interpretation. To help the public (and especially the legal profession) understand various examples of uses that have been deemed fair or not fair, the Copyright Office has created a searchable database of court opinions called the Fair Use Index; it is available at copyright.gov/fair-use/.

The fair use provisions of copyright law are so nonspecific that most lawyers categorically consider fair use to be a gray area. The law does *not* specify word limits or percentages that do or do not qualify as fair use. Rather, the law calls for the following four factors to be taken into consideration:

> 1. The purpose and character of the use, including whether such use is of commercial nature or is for nonprofit educational purposes
> 2. The nature of the copyrighted work

> 3. The amount and substantiality of the portion used in relation to the copyrighted work as a whole
> 4. The effect of the use upon the potential market for, or value of, the copyrighted work

As you can see, the third factor in the fair use rubric is the length of the selection to be used and its relation to the length of the work as a whole. It is because of this factor that publishers often operate with fair use guidelines expressed in terms of quantity.

Although a set of guidelines based on word counts is straightforward and easy for permissions editors to apply, it may result in the publisher paying for permissions that didn't need to be requested. At least that's the view of some lawyers and other experts, who argue that when a use is "transformative," it addresses the first and fourth factors in the four-factor fair use rubric. According to this view, if an author has used copyrighted material in a highly creative way that transforms the original work and gives it new meaning, the use is likely to qualify as fair. Compared to a word count, this "transformative" standard is a highly subjective judgment that would require a great deal of time and effort on the part of the publisher in examining each individual case. This is probably why, in more than thirty years of working with permissions, I personally have never seen a publisher use the "transformative" standard to justify deeming a use "fair."

Another term used by some publishers, primarily those based in the UK, is "fair dealing." In contrast to fair use, which is the law of the land in the United States, fair dealing is an international principle that relies on whether the copyrighted material is used for purposes of "review and criticism." The idea is that the author should use only as much of the copyrighted work as is necessary to illustrate the point being made in the discussion, and it assumes that the discussion pertains to the copyrighted work.

For example, if I am discussing popular music of the 1960s and I quote a line from a Beatles song (with attribution to the source), my use may qualify as fair dealing. If I am writing about the properties of psychoactive drugs and I quote a line from a Beatles song because I think it describes what it feels like to be under the influence of a drug, it's less certain that this would be fair dealing, even if I gave full attribution to the source, because my review and criticism is related to psychoactive drugs, not to the Beatles or their music. If I am writing a novel and want to quote a line from a Beatles song as a way of setting the mood for, say, a love scene in which the lovers use drugs, it's highly doubtful that this would be fair dealing because I am not providing any review or criticism of the Beatles song, I am merely using the lyrics to enhance the aesthetics of my novel.

Patent, Trademark, Privacy, and Libel

Issues of copyright sometimes overlap with the other two major forms of intellectual property law: patent and trademark. Although patent and trademark are similar to copyright in that they allow the originator of something to control and be compensated for the entity he or she has originated, they differ from copyright in many ways. In a nutshell, patents protect devices and processes; for an invention to qualify for a patent, it has to be shown to function or to accomplish the purpose for which it is intended. Trademarks and service marks are a form of branding—a way of identifying and distinguishing the source of a given product or service from other, similar products or services. The United States Patent and Trademark Office is the best place to start in obtaining further details about patents and trademarks: uspto.gov/.

Issues of privacy and libel may also come into play in the course of working with copyright. Again, these can be related to copyright in that they involve a person's being able to control what belongs to them: in this case, the person's privacy or good name. Privacy law (in a nutshell) deals with the "right to be left alone," the right to keep personal facts private, and protection against identity theft. Libel deals with protection against having one's reputation defamed by the malicious publication of false information.

Patent, trademark, privacy, and libel are all complex areas of the legal system, which even the most experienced permissions editor could not be expected to handle. However, the knowledge about copyright and permissions provided in this book should be helpful in determining when a lawyer may be needed to help resolve an issue related to any or all of these areas of the law.

ELSA PETERSON

How Long Does Copyright Protection Last?

The duration of United States copyright protection changed dramatically in October 1998 when President Bill Clinton signed into law the Copyright Term Extension Act, spearheaded by the late congressman and entertainer Sonny Bono and therefore referred to as the Sonny Bono Copyright Term Extension Act (SBCTEA). This law, which took effect immediately, extended the duration of copyright protection for any works then under copyright, and for all works subsequently copyrighted, for an additional twenty years.

Two decades before the SBCTEA, Congress passed a different piece of legislation that signaled a sea change in the duration of copyright protection. The Copyright Act of 1976, which took effect on January 1, 1978, overturned nearly two centuries of United States legal tradition by tying copyright duration to the date of creation and the life of the creator, rather than to the date of publication. By that law, works created on or after January 1, 1978, received protection for the life of the creator plus fifty years. The SBCTEA continued this principle for works created from 1978, but extended the duration to the life of the creator plus seventy years.

What about works created or published before 1978? The duration of copyright for those works is still counted from the date of publication, not the author's life span—but it runs for ninety-five years instead of the previous seventy-five years. The SBCTEA also extends protection for unpublished works, works of corporate authorship, and other categories of copyrighted material. The legislation can be viewed at the Library of Congress Copyright Office website at loc.gov/copyright/legislation/s505.pdf.

There are further complexities to United States copyright duration, notably for unpublished works, works of corporate authorship, compilations, anonymous and pseudonymous works, and other atypical types of intellectual property. In addition, because pre-1978 law required copyrights to be renewed after twenty-eight years, some material that was published after 1923 has fallen into the public domain because its copyright was not renewed. The renewal requirement was abolished for works published after 1963. Therefore, a work that was first published between 1923 and 1963 is no longer protected unless copyright has been renewed. Copyright Office Circular 15a, *Duration of Copyright*, deals with this topic; it is available at copyright.gov/circs/.

How can you tell whether copyright to a work was renewed or not? The Library of Congress does not have a way of searching for renewals online. However, the Stanford University Libraries have compiled an online database of renewals received by the United States Copyright Office for books published in the United States between 1923 and 1963. The Stanford Copyright Renewal Database is accessible at: tinyurl.com/325e3p or collections.stanford.edu/copyrightrenewals/bin/page?forward=home.

It is important to be aware that if you are interested in a work that is not a book, was not published in the United States, or was not published between 1923 and 1963, it will not appear in the Stanford Copyright Renewal Database. To search for such a work, you would need to examine Copyright Office records, and this requires a trip to Washington, DC, to visit the Copyright Records Reading Room in person. If your budget does not allow for such a trip, you can place a request for the Library of Congress staff to perform a search. This involves only a modest fee, but it usually takes several weeks, if not months, so it is not a viable option for a project on a tight production schedule. A more efficient solution may be to hire a freelancer in the Washington, DC, area to perform the search. (Let's hear it for freelancers!)

Table 1 is a brief summary of the duration of copyright protection under the new and old rules, for material created or first published on various dates.

Table 1. The duration of copyright protection

Publication date	Prior protection	New protection under SBCTEA
1922 or earlier	75 years (now public domain [PD])	Same: now PD
1923–1963	75 years if renewed; 28 if not renewed (now PD)	95 years if renewed; 28 if not renewed (now PD)
1964–1977	75 years	95 years
1978 or later	Starts when created, continues through life of creator plus 50 years	Starts when created, continues through life of creator plus 70 years

To this point, we've discussed only United States copyright law. Copyright laws in other countries differ in a number of ways, notably in the duration of copyright. Throughout most of the world, copyright duration has traditionally been tied to the life of the creator plus a certain number of years, just as it now is in the United States. And in most of Europe and South America, the rule is life plus 70 years—the same rule the United States now uses for works published from 1978 onward. However, in some countries the term is considerably shorter, and in others it is longer. Mexico, at life plus 100 years, has the longest copyright protection of any major country. Because publishers in the United States often seek Canadian rights, it is important to know that Canadian copyright duration is life plus 50 years.

The foregoing discussion of what copyright is and how it works has primarily relied on the historical and traditional functions of copyright in publishing. In the next part of this book, the focus will shift to newer developments that have arisen as technology has brought major challenges to copyright. The law has struggled to keep pace.

PART II:

COPYRIGHT IN THE TWENTY-FIRST CENTURY

Life has changed remarkably since 1999 and so have copyright and permissions. Think of how we use media today, and recall that in 1999 the vast majority of our reading material consisted of newspapers, magazines, and books printed on paper. Online booksellers were a newfangled experiment, and ebooks were nearly impossible to read and even harder to download. Authors wrote their manuscripts on computers, but editing was generally done with pencil and paper. Web searches were slow and frustrating. The Copyright Office accepted registration applications only on paper, and just a few of the most forward-looking publishers would accept permission requests via fax. Email had caught on, but only the "digerati" embraced such novelties as texting and blogs, and Facebook and Twitter had not yet been introduced. Cell phones, personal digital music players, pocket-size "digital assistant" computers, and portable digital game devices were all separate items; there was no such thing as a smartphone.

While this book cannot begin to cover all the ways in which copyright has changed since the dawn of the twenty-first century, the topics discussed are intended to give a sense of where we came from, how we got to where we are now, and where we're headed.

The Digital Millennium Copyright Act

In 1998 Congress passed the Digital Millennium Copyright Act (DMCA), which clarifies that copyright protection is in no way diminished by virtue of a material's being digital, electronic, internet-based, or the like. The DMCA defends the anti-piracy measures built into most commercial software, making it a crime to circumvent such measures. It also seeks to balance the need to exchange information with the need to protect copyright in a digital environment, for example, by exempting online service providers from liability for copyright infringements committed by users who post copyrighted material on their sites. The full text of the DMCA is available from the Copyright Office at: tinyurl.com/75mkadh or copyright.gov/legislation/dmca.pdf.

The DMCA is perhaps the most far-reaching of several pieces of copyright legislation intended to close loopholes and address complexities that emerged as evolving technology advanced beyond the restrictions of existing laws. Other examples are the No Electronic Theft Act of 1997, the Digital Audio Home Recording Act of 1992, and the Technology, Education, and Copyright Harmonization (TEACH) Act of 2002.

Social Media

Email, texting, Twitter, blogs, Facebook, MySpace, LinkedIn, YouTube, Flickr, and other means of electronic sharing have made it easier than ever to infringe on the copyrights of others. And to have one's own material infringed on. A generation ago, if I wanted to quote an excerpt from a copyrighted work in a manuscript I was composing, I had to type the quotation verbatim from a photocopy, or even write it painstakingly by hand on 3″ x 5″ cards in the library. Today, of course, I would be able to copy and paste directly from a website or, if the website was encrypted, I could take a screenshot, paste it, strip out the formatting, and repurpose the content. It's so easy to take other people's content, it's as if copyright law were a naive note stuck to an unattended wallet left out on a park bench: "This is my wallet and if you take money out of it you'll be breaking the law."

Copyright and Permissions

If you have ever looked at the section on any social networking website labeled "Terms of Service," "Terms of Use," or simply "Terms," you know that these terms are fairly complex. It's a safe bet that most people have not read the user agreement for any of the social media they routinely use. Instead, people go ahead and use these communication tools with a set of intuitive ethics in mind. This works fairly well most of the time, just as driving in a foreign country without knowing the traffic laws may work fairly well, as long as you basically know how to drive.

The DMCA and related court decisions have established that online service providers are not liable for infringement committed by users who post copyrighted material without permission. Moreover, most social networking terms of use state that users are responsible for all content they upload or post. This clearly means that, if I use someone else's copyrighted material in an online environment without permission, I am the one breaking the law. Yet people do this all the time, don't they? Most of the time, when people do this in informal venues like social media sites, the originators of the material don't object. If someone does object to a social media posting, they can ask that it be taken down. Depending on the Terms of Use, the offender may have the right to appeal, and the service provider may reserve the right to decide who prevails in a conflict between users. Although minor infractions of this nature can be sticky, they are usually resolved without anyone having to go to court.

For editorial freelancers, questions of digital copyright take on greater importance when a project depends on the client's ability to use material from a social networking site. Consider some examples of screenshots that nonfiction authors might want to use:

- a Twitter feed as an example of concise writing in an English composition manual
- a Facebook page as an example of how people form and maintain relationships in a sociology text
- a page from an online dating site as an example of mate selection in a book about human sexuality
- an online Spanish-language advertisement for an internet service provider as an example of bilingualism in American society

- a *Washington Post* live chat transcript about healthcare legislation as an example of opinion leadership
- a personal blog entry about one family's difficulties in obtaining health insurance as an example of how public policy affects individuals

Which of these, if any, require permission? If permission is required, would permission from the web host (Twitter, Facebook, dating site, etc.) be sufficient? Or would the requestor have to contact the individuals who posted the tweets, the person whose Facebook page is being used, the dating candidates profiled on the dating site, and/or the authors of the blogs?

The answer to all of these questions comes down to the fine print in the Terms of Use section of the website in question. Let's explore Facebook as an example. According to the Terms at facebook.com/legal/terms?ref=pf (as of April 2020):

> You own the intellectual property rights (things like copyright or trademarks) in any such content that you create and share on Facebook and the other Facebook Company Products you use. Nothing in these Terms takes away the rights you have to your own content. You are free to share your content with anyone else, wherever you want.
>
> ...
>
> Specifically, when you share, post, or upload content that is covered by intellectual property rights on or in connection with our Products, you grant us a non-exclusive, transferable, sub-licensable, royalty-free, and worldwide license to host, use, distribute, modify, run, copy, publicly perform or display, translate, and create derivative works of your content (consistent with your privacy and application settings). This means, for example, that if you share a photo on Facebook, you give us permission to store, copy, and share it with others (again, consistent with your settings) such as service providers that support our service or other Facebook Products you use. This license will end when your content is deleted from our systems.

As an experienced permissions editor (but not a lawyer), I interpret this to mean that Facebook does not have the right to grant permission for a third party to reproduce someone's entire Facebook page. However, if the would-be user was not interested in using an entire Facebook screenshot but merely a series of photographs from a Facebook page, Facebook would have the right to grant the use of the photographs. This is not to say that they would do this, but according to my reading of their Terms, they could.

The responses to the other examples above can be addressed, similarly, by reading the Terms of the online host in question. If you're the type of person who enjoys drilling down and reading fine print, permissions editing may be just the career for you!

One other point needs to be mentioned with regard to screenshots of social media pages: they tend to include advertisements and other pieces of content that may be owned by entirely different entities than the owner of the "main" content the author wants to show. For example, an author may care about the content of a *Washington Post* live chat transcript, but not about the banner advertisement for Sheraton hotels displayed across the top of the screen. The author also may not care about the logos for Facebook, YouTube, and Twitter that appear on the screen. Nevertheless, if that particular screenshot is to be used, permission needs to be cleared for the Sheraton ad as well as for those corporate logos, and the *Washington Post* is very unlikely to be able to provide those clearances. This is just one example of the many complexities facing writers and editors when it comes to digital rights and social media.

Digital Collaboration

Unlike online social networking, collaborative work has a long history in copyright law. Throughout the centuries, people have collaborated to write fiction and nonfiction, to create works of visual art, to compose music, and so on. Library of Congress copyright registration forms have had space for multiple authors since at least the days of the typewriter. Recall the example of the poem on the cocktail napkin that I gave under "How Is Copyright Established?" If I write the poem, my husband draws the sketch, my sister takes the photograph, and my nephew shoots the video, we now have a video that is a joint work involving four creators. And we know how to contact all four of the creators if someone wants permission to use that video for some other purpose. This is not new.

What is new in the twenty-first century is digital collaboration. Digital collaboration is made possible by software that seamlessly merges the contributions of many users, often without a means of tracking who contributed what. Sometimes known as groupware or wikis, these software platforms are popular in the workplace, where all users with access to the platform are employed by the company assigning the work.

You might say digital collaboration is like "free love" among consenting adults. As long as everyone involved knows what they're getting into and agrees to it, why not? The problem arises when someone decides they want to claim copyright to work created in a cloud or wiki.

Suppose, for example, that an artist wants to take a three-minute video capture of a live Twitter feed as the words move along the screen, and incorporate this moving image into a multimedia work of art. A Twitter feed is like a wiki in the sense of being a digital collaboration: dozens of Twitter users have posted tweets in the three minutes covered by the video. Can the artist use these tweets without permission? If permission is needed, would permission from Twitter suffice? Or would the artist need to contact every Twitter contributor whose tweet appeared during the three minutes? What about retweets—would the original Twitter user have to give permission in addition to the person who retweeted the tweet?

We can answer these questions by reading the Twitter website's Terms of Service at twitter.com/en/tos (accessed 6/1/20). Under "Your Rights and Grant of Rights in the Content," we find the following.

> You retain your rights to any Content you submit, post or display on or through the Services. What's yours is yours — you own your Content (and your incorporated audio, photos and videos are considered part of the Content).
>
> By submitting, posting or displaying Content on or through the Services, you grant us a worldwide, non-exclusive, royalty-free license (with the right to sublicense) to use, copy, reproduce,

process, adapt, modify, publish, transmit, display and distribute such Content in any and all media or distribution methods now known or later developed (for clarity, these rights include, for example, curating, transforming, and translating). This license authorizes us to make your Content available to the rest of the world and to let others do the same.

Further, under "Your License to Use the Services," we find that:

The Services [provided by Twitter] are protected by copyright, trademark, and other laws of both the United States and other countries. Nothing in the Terms gives you a right to use the Twitter name or any of the Twitter trademarks, logos, domain names, other distinctive brand features, and other proprietary rights. All right, title, and interest in and to the Services (excluding Content provided by users) are and will remain the exclusive property of Twitter and its licensors.

Emphasizing once again that I am an experienced permissions editor but not a lawyer, I interpret this to mean that Twitter would have the right to license the tweets to the artist, and that Twitter contributors would not have the right to be contacted for permission or to receive credit beyond whatever screen name or other "branding" appears publicly in their tweets. To my knowledge, no case like this has yet arisen, but it's easy to imagine that somewhere in the world, some creative person is experimenting with works of this very nature. I hope this example will be helpful in illustrating some of the implications of digital collaboration with regard to copyright.

Google Books and the Internet Archive

In 2004, the search engine company Google announced an agreement with several major libraries to digitize millions of books and make them available online. Many of these books were in the public domain, but others were protected by copyright. Some were "orphan works"—that is, their rights holders could not be located. Others were out of print, and still others were copyrighted books that are in print and whose authors are alive and easy to contact. Google argued that this scheme was legal under the fair use doctrine of the copyright law (see the section on fair use in Part I).

Objections were raised by hundreds of authors, publishers, and organizations, led by the Authors Guild and the Association of American Publishers (AAP). Soon a lawsuit was filed against Google and gained class-action status. For some time it looked like the parties might agree to a settlement—but after years of legal wrangling, on November 14, 2013, US District Court Judge Denny Chin issued a ruling dismissing the lawsuit; he opined that Google's use of the works was fair use according to the four-factors rubric in copyright law. Among other reasons, he said "Google's digitization was 'transformative,' meaning it gave the books a new purpose or character, and could be expected to boost rather than reduce book sales." The plaintiffs appealed, and the case made its way all the way to the US Supreme Court. However, on April 18, 2016 the court denied the petition, leaving the ruling in Google's favor intact.

In the meantime, another organization called the Internet Archive (or IA) began offering public access to a wide variety of material: books, newspaper and magazine articles, audio, moving images, works of art, and web-based content, among other types (see https://archive.org/index.php). IA is a 501(c)3 not-for-profit entity, supported by dozens of charitable and philanthropic organizations, with a mission of "universal access to all knowledge" (see https://archive.org/about/). IA's book digitization project entails physically obtaining books and running them through scanners; it operates more than two dozen scanning facilities in multiple foreign countries, with the capability of scanning 1,000 books per day.

IA argues that it has the right to share portions of copyrighted books and other copyrighted works under a principle they call "controlled digital lending," which allows users to "borrow" the material digitally for a limited period of time; or, if the item is in the public domain, users can download it permanently. According to IA's terms of use, "Access to the Archive's Collections is provided at no cost to you and is granted for scholarship and research purposes only."

Despite IA's stated aim to help people who can't afford to buy books or pay for movie downloads ("Not everyone has access to a public or academic library with a good collection . . ."), its critics argue that IA is undercutting the ability of writers and other creators to earn a living from their copyrighted works. In June 2020, four major publishing companies filed a lawsuit against the Internet Archive, alleging "'willful mass infringement' of copyrights by scanning books and distributing copies on the OpenLibrary.org and Archive.org websites, without any permission from, or payment to, the publishers or authors of the works included in those books." It remains to be seen whether this litigation will be more successful than the Google Books lawsuit was.

Is Copyright Obsolete?

As mentioned earlier, the United States Constitution established copyright for the purpose of "promot[ing] the Progress of Science and the useful Arts." Like many portions of the Constitution, this clause has been a subject of debate as legal scholars, legislators, and representatives of "science and the useful arts" exchange views on how copyright can continue to serve its purpose today.

Some argue that copyright is an obsolete concept: because copying and borrowing other people's material is so ridiculously easy in a digital environment, no one should try to stop others from copying and borrowing one's material. Others believe that freely sharing material with others is a moral obligation: a way of contributing to society in which learning is encouraged, thus leading to better scholarship and furthering knowledge.

These views are fundamental to the Creative Commons online project. Creative Commons takes the traditional "all rights reserved" approach to copyright and transforms it into what it calls "some rights reserved." According to its home page, Creative Commons is "dedicated to building a globally-accessible public commons of knowledge and culture. We make it easier for people to share their creative and academic work, as well as to access and build upon the work of others." To this end, Creative Commons offers a range of licenses that streamline the process for individuals and organizations to allow their material to be used within certain limits, without any permission fee, while still retaining their copyrights. Table 2 summarizes available licenses (as of April 2020) and their meaning.

Table 2. Creative Commons licenses

Attribution (CC BY)	My work may be freely used and adapted, and I must be given credit.
Attribution ShareAlike (CC BY-SA)	My work may be freely used and adapted, provided that the user also allows the resulting work to be freely used and adapted by others, and I must be given credit.
Attribution-NoDerivs (CC BY-ND)	My work may be freely used, but may not be adapted or changed in any way, and I must be given credit.
Attribution-NonCommercial (CC BY-NC)	My work may be freely used and adapted, but only by noncommercial users, and I must be given credit.
Attribution-NonCommercial-ShareAlike (CC BY-NC-SA)	My work may be freely used and adapted, but only by noncommercial users, provided that the user also allows the resulting work to be freely used and adapted by others, and I must be given credit.
Attribution-NonCommercial-NoDerivs (CC BY-NC-ND)	My work may be freely used, but only by noncommercial users, and it may not be adapted or changed in any way, and I must be given credit.

A helpful essay describing and explaining these licenses, their uses, and the philosophy behind them is available at creativecommons.org/licenses/. For those seeking a higher level of expertise in this field, Creative Commons also offers certification courses. In partnership with the American Library Association, Creative Commons has authored a book, *Creative Commons for Educators and Librarians*, that explains how to "make the most of the Open Access (OA) and open educational resources (OER) movements." It is available for download at certificates.creative-commons.org/about/certificate-resources-cc-by/.

The Creative Commons ShareAlike provision is related to the concept of "copyleft." Copyleft, which is most often used for open-source software and other information technology, involves giving away the right to reproduce and adapt one's material provided that the user will, in turn, give it away and never attempt to claim copyright or profit from the resulting work. Because copyleft promotes a chain reaction of users giving away their material, it can also be called viral licensing.

Creative Commons licenses and copyleft do not release a work from copyright altogether. To do that, an author might place an "anti-copyright" notice on the work with wording such as "Anti-copyright. Copy and distribute this work freely. You don't have to credit the source." Or, in more formal language, "The author hereby waives all claim of copyright for this work and places it in the public domain."

The problem with a blanket release or waiver of this type is that it does not prevent someone else from claiming copyright and profiting from one's material. If the copyright expires on a known work (a Mark Twain novel, for example), the work becomes available for adaptation, and those adaptations can be copyrighted, but the Mark Twain novel itself is still in the public domain. In contrast, with a newly created work, waiving copyright puts the author in a bind because it would be extremely difficult to defend against someone else's claim of copyright.

As an example, say I am an unknown musician (which, actually, I am), and I've written a song that I want to make freely available for people to sing, record, write down, and distribute as sheet music. If I affix an anti-copyright notice or waiver to my YouTube video of my song, some famous musician could hear it, like it, decide to record it, claim copyright, and deny me any credit or profits from the sale of the recording. Because I have recorded my song, which constitutes fixing it in tangible form under the law, it might be possible for me to defend my copyright against this usurpation. However, because my tangible form also includes a notice waiving copyright, it's questionable whether I would have a legal leg to stand on. Even if I did have a case, pursuing that kind of legal action would be a major headache. It is for reasons such as these that I will argue that for as long as we have copyright laws and as long as users are willing to pay for copyrighted material, copyright is not obsolete.

Will the Duration of Copyright Be Extended?

When the Sonny Bono Copyright Term Extension Act (SBCTEA) was passed in 1998, it was not without controversy. Some of its strongest supporters were large entertainment companies whose copyrights included classic movies from the 1920s and 1930s. With the then-existing term for works of corporate authorship at seventy-five years, these movies would have gone into the public domain in the early twenty-first century. The first film starring Mickey Mouse, for example, was produced in 1928 and would have gone into the public domain in 2003 had the duration of copyright not been extended. The Walt Disney Company's intense lobbying in favor of SBCTEA gave the law the nickname of "The Mickey Mouse Protection Act."

On the other hand, critics charged that life plus seventy years, or ninety-five years for a work of corporate authorship, would stifle creativity by placing unreasonable controls on old works that should have been allowed to fall into the public domain. Some predicted that when the ninety-five-year copyright "clock" was about to start moving again in 2018, a movement would again arise to extend copyright. If Mickey Mouse could be protected for ninety-five years, why not 115 years, or 125 years?

Indeed, the trend throughout the twentieth century was toward increasingly longer copyright protection. From twenty-eight years (1909) with a second twenty-eight-year renewal, to the life of the creator plus fifty years (1976), to the life of the creator plus seventy years (1998), the pattern was clear. But in the twenty-first century, there has been little political appetite to continue this trend. As of January 1, 2019, the copyright "clock" did indeed start moving, and numerous well-known films, literary works, and musical compositions fell into the public domain. Here are just a few examples:

Copyright and Permissions

- *The City Without Jews* (Die Stadt ohne Juden) by Hans Karl Breslauer (2020)
- *The Gift of Black Folk* by W. E. B. Du Bois (2020)
- *A Passage to India* by E. M. Forster (2020)
- *Rhapsody in Blue* by George Gershwin (2020)
- *The Ten Commandments* directed by Cecil B. DeMille (2019)
- *Tulips and Chimneys* by E. E. Cummings (2019)
- *Twenty Love Poems and a Song of Despair* (Veinte poemas de amor y una canción desesperada) by Pablo Neruda (2020)
- *Violin Sonata No. 1* and *Violin Sonata No. 2* by Béla Bartók
- *The World Crisis* by Winston S. Churchill (2019)
- *Yes! We Have No Bananas* by Frank Silver & Irving Cohn (2019)

At what point will The Walt Disney Company and other holders of lucrative copyrights decide that a given copyright duration is long enough? Or will they be unable to persuade enough members of Congress to enact another term extension? Time will tell.

PART III:
GUIDE TO PERMISSIONS EDITING

On the surface, clearing permissions might seem like a purely clerical task, one that could be accomplished by just about anyone who knows how to fill in the fields in an online application form. This view of permissions is probably the reason why quite a few authors are willing to enter into book contracts that require authors to handle their own permissions. Authors of books that include a lot of preexisting material, such as college textbooks, which typically have dozens if not a hundred or more permission items, may live to regret this decision.

A permissions project can quickly become a nightmare if the person doing it doesn't know the tricks of the trade, which are what you will learn in this section. To be a good permissions editor, one needs more than top-notch clerical skills. The job also involves detective work, communicating effectively with total strangers, negotiating fees, and diplomacy in dealing with clients and rights holders. And, of course, a good permissions editor will be knowledgeable about the ins and outs of copyright as applied to the project at hand.

What Is Permissions Editing?

Permissions editing is the obtaining of copyright clearances for the reuse of preexisting material, including text (prose and poetry), artwork (charts and graphs, cartoons, rendered drawings, etc.), musical notation, and any other type of work the author may have chosen for inclusion. If the project is a digital publication, it may also contain nonprint preexisting material such as audio recordings, video or film clips, computer art, and other digital media.

Permissions editing can also include photographs, but for much of the twentieth century photo editing was a freelance specialty separate from permissions editing. This has changed in the digital era as more and more publishing projects include screen captures, digitally created art, video stills from advertisements, and a host of other items that do not fit neatly into either the "photo" or "text" category. In my experience, the trend has been for photo editors to be responsible only for images that can be obtained from photo agencies, photographers, and fine art sources such as museums. "Text" permissions editors, for their part, are usually responsible for clearances of all other categories of material.

Publishers usually hire the permissions editor for a project about the time a manuscript is turned over to production, although occasionally an author may turn to a freelancer in desperation after spending several increasingly frustrating weeks trying to clear permissions without the help of a professional. What both of these situations have in common is that the manuscript is complete and the book is on a production schedule with a publisher.

Occasionally a freelancer will be approached by an author who wants permissions cleared even though the project has not yet been signed with a publisher. The only reasonable response in that situation is: "I can't accept your money under these circumstances, but I'd be delighted if you would recommend me when you get a publishing contract."

There are two good reasons for this. First, a manuscript without a publisher is likely to undergo substantial editing changes after a publisher signs it, and it would be a waste of time and effort to seek permission for material that might end up being deleted from the manuscript. Second, and more to the point, rights holders will need to be told who will be publishing the book, and when, before they can consider a permission request.

The following section describes the basics of how permissions editing is done, beginning with the four necessary steps in a typical permissions project.

Four Basic Steps in Permissions Editing

Almost any permissions editing project will require examining the manuscript to determine what needs permission, building the database, contacting rights holders, and providing the publisher with acknowledgments or credits. Each of these steps will be discussed in detail.

Step 1: Examining the Manuscript

Permissions editing begins with an examination of the manuscript (or, if the product is nonprint, the script, dub tape, storyboard, shot sheet, etc.) with the goal of identifying all the preexisting material embedded in it that will need clearance. Although the client is usually the main contact for the project, the permissions editor should take advantage of any opportunity to communicate directly with the author because the author can be very helpful in making sure that all preexisting material is designated as such. For example, quoted excerpts should be set off in quotation marks or in indented block paragraphs, and the author needs to bring any preexisting material that is *not* set off in this way to the editor's attention.

While benefiting from author input, permissions editors should not fail to exercise their own professional judgment. Authors have been known to make erroneous assumptions about the need for permission or lack thereof, ranging from "I don't remember where I got that, but let's just use it anyway" to "I'm sure he won't mind my quoting from his article; he's a friend of mine."

In addition to clarifying which material comes from preexisting sources, the author should also alert the permissions editor to any material that is paraphrased, adapted, or otherwise modified from the original. In some cases, adaptations are different enough from the original to be considered original or synthesized, but this is a judgment that should usually be made by the client, not the permissions editor. The permissions editor's role with modified preexisting material is to query the client and find out whether the client deems permission necessary; deems the material sufficiently modified to be considered the author's own work; or wants to direct the author to rework the material, either to use it in non-modified form or to modify it sufficiently that it can be deemed the author's own. In considering modified preexisting material, it is important to keep in mind that some rights holders refuse to permit any modifications, no matter how minor or how necessary for the intended audience. Other rights holders are relatively liberal in their willingness to allow modifications.

Sometimes the initial step of examining the manuscript and flagging permission items is performed in-house by the client. If that is the case, the freelance permissions editor should still query any items that look like they would require permission that the client hasn't flagged, and any that are flagged that look like they should not require permission. Of course, since the client is paying for the freelancer's services, the final decision about what needs permission is up to the client.

Not all preexisting material needs formal permission. There are two major categories of material that may be used without permission: public domain and fair use. These were discussed earlier under "Public Domain and Fair Use."

To reiterate, material in the public domain is material not protected by copyright. Material is in the public domain if it was first published more than ninety-five years ago, is a United States government publication, has a copyright that was never renewed, or was created prior to 1978 and never published or never copyrighted.

While the first two conditions on this list are fairly straightforward, it can be very difficult to tell whether a copyright was renewed; or, even more so, if a work was never published or copyrighted. If a client really wants to use material whose copyright status is unclear, and does not want to take a chance on being sued for infringement, it may be necessary to search for a copyright registration or renewal. This process was explained under "How Long Does Copyright Protection Last?" If a work published before 1978 was never registered, or if it required a renewal and was not renewed, then it is in the public domain and it may be used, abridged, translated, or adapted without permission and without credit to the source, although for pedagogical or ethical reasons credit is usually given.

The second category of material that does not require formal permission, fair use, was also discussed under "Public Domain and Fair Use." As mentioned there, publishers generally use word limits for their fair use guidelines. For example, one publisher may consider as fair use up to 500 words from a book; 100 words from a short story, essay, or article; and two or more figures or tables. Another publisher may require permission clearance for anything exceeding 200 words from a book; fifty words from a short story, essay, or article; and for all figures and tables.

Beginning around 2010, a number of leading publishers adopted stricter fair use guidelines than they had previously used, so that even very short excerpts were subject to formal permission. This has been quite frustrating for authors of books undergoing revision because quoted material that was used in previous editions of a book without permission (but with attribution to the source) now involves not only the cost of seeking permission but also the risk of incurring a substantial permission fee or even having the permission denied. But, again, these are decisions made by the client who hires the freelancer: the saying "The customer is always right" applies here.

At the outset of the project, a permissions editor should always ask the client for a clear explanation of the fair use guidelines applicable to the project because the scope of the project and the amount of work involved will depend on how liberal or strict the client's policy is.

Step 2: Building the Database

Many clients either recommend or require that their freelance permissions editors use a certain format for a permissions database or log. If the project is a revision of a publication for which permissions were cleared in the previous edition, the client can often provide the permission records from the previous edition, but they are not always available. The permissions database or log the client provides may be an Excel spreadsheet, a Word table, or a web-based data entry form. If the client does not provide this, the freelancer should create one that includes, at a minimum, the fields or data categories shown in Table 3.

Table 3. Building the permissions database

Field name	Information to enter in field
Manuscript page	The location in the manuscript where the permission item (the material for which permission will be sought) is found
Description	Identification of the permission item with as many details as possible, including author, title, date, word count of the excerpt to be used, and any other identifying details given in the manuscript
Rights holder	Name of publisher, website, or other source where the permission item was previously published, with space for contact details to be filled in when the permissions editor researches them
Actions taken	Dates of first contact and medium of contact (email, fax, website "Contact" page, etc.), first formal request, second request, any informal assurance that permission is on its way, etc.
Granted	Date granted and medium of clearance (signed letter emailed as PDF, signed letter via postal mail, rights holder's own contract, etc.)
Credit	Wording of acknowledgment as specified by the rights holder
Fee	In United States dollars or foreign currency; any fee breakdown by format or territory
Comp copies	Number of complimentary copies, if any, required as a condition of the permission
Rights conveyed	All editions or just the current edition; format (hardcover, paperback, any electronic formats), territory, any calendar time limit, any other rights granted, and any other restrictions
Comments	A useful space for anything that does not fit into the other fields

Note that although the above list of fields is formatted vertically, in a working database they would be laid out horizontally in Landscape format so that a large number of permission items can be entered in rows. Table 4 is an example:

Table 4. A working database

Ms. page	Description	Rights holder	Actions taken	Granted	Credit	Fee	Comp copies	Rights conveyed	Comments
005	Surname of author, first name. "Title of Poem" from *Title of Book*. # of words quoted.	Random House							
042	Surname of author, first initial (date). title of article. *Title of Psychological Journal*, page. # of words quoted.	American Psychological Association							
101	Surname of artist, first name. Title of painting. Date. Museum Collection.	Art Resource, New York							

The database or log will be the freelancer's workbench for the project, so it is important to set it up with care and forethought. It is helpful to continually ask oneself, *if X happens, how will I indicate this in my log?* Also consider that the beauty of a database is its ability to sort by category, but sorting works only when the data is entered in a consistent fashion. For example, if the permission items are to be sorted by author, the first word in the Description field should always be the surname of the author of the permission item, and if no author is known, a placeholder such as "Author TBD" or "Anonymous" will be needed.

Perhaps the most important category for sorting is the name of the rights holder, because if the project includes excerpts from several different publications belonging to the same rights holder, these should all be requested together. Rights holders may get annoyed if they receive requests piecemeal, so it is important to be consistent in how the name is entered, such that sorting the database will bring all the relevant entries into one series.

Step 3: Contacting Copyright Holders

In most cases the rights holder is the publisher of the material; at least that is the place to start. If the manuscript includes an excerpt from a book, for example, then you will place a request with the publisher of that book. The publisher may end up referring you to the author's literary agent, but you won't know whether the agent has the right to handle the permission unless the publisher tells you so. The contact information for publishers (and for any other rights holder that has a website) is usually fairly easy to find. The first step is to examine the company's website. Some sites have a specific link for permissions. More typically, the information about how to request permission is located under Contact Us, Licensing, Legal, or Terms of Use.

But what if the manuscript includes excerpts from material that is unpublished, or out of print, or whose publisher has gone out of business? That's when the fun begins. The internet has made it easier than ever before to find people and businesses, especially those that have a reasonably distinctive name. Names like "Mary Johnson" or "Carlos Garcia" are slightly more challenging, but an online search that comes up dry is not the end of the story. Is the rights holder's last known address located in a small town? Perhaps a reference librarian in the town's library knows something about the person or company. Is the rights holder an individual active in a given academic discipline? If so, they probably belong to that discipline's professional organization, such as the American Psychological Association or the American Musicological Society. During the search for a copyright holder, it is important to keep a record of the sources attempted so that if the search does prove fruitless there will be a record that the permissions editor made a good-faith effort.

For some rights holders, the only means of initiating contact is a "Contact Us" field on their website. In using this field for an initial inquiry, it is important to state clearly and concisely that you are working for a publisher and want to submit a copyright permission request. Consider:

> I am a freelance editor clearing permissions for a book to be published this year by XX Publisher. We wish to use an excerpt from one of your publications. Please let me know the person or department to whom I may submit a formal request giving the full details of our proposed use. Thank you.

Compare that with "What is your email address and phone number? I would like to contact you for a project I am working on." Which one would you take seriously and answer promptly?

Other rights holders have a web-based permission request procedure with a form that the freelancer must fill out online. The permission request page can usually be found with a certain amount of persistence by drilling down in the website of the publisher or other rights holder. Here are a few examples of permission request pages.

- Pearson: pearsoned.com/wp-content/uploads/Request-for-Reprint-Permission.pdf
- Random House: permissions.penguinrandomhouse.com/
- University of Michigan Press: press.umich.edu/script/press/contact/reprint
- Hal Leonard (song lyrics): halleonard.com/licensing/pre_lyric_request.jsp

Another resource permissions editors will want to be familiar with is the Copyright Clearance Center (CCC), which handles permissions on behalf of a great many academic journals as well as some publishers and other organizations. It functions as one-stop shopping for many kinds of uses. Requesting permission through CCC is a bit of a challenge for a freelancer because the CCC's default assumption is that the requestor is also the user. Based on this assumption, when CCC grants a permission, an invoice is generated making the requestor responsible for paying the permission fee. CCC, however, does include options for a freelancer to indicate that the request is on behalf of a third party. In this case the client, rather than the freelancer, is named as the responsible party on the CCC invoice. It can be a challenge to navigate through the CCC online requesting process, but the good news is that once you have filled out all the fields correctly, permission is typically granted in a matter of minutes if not seconds.

Apart from these online fill-in communication channels, a permission request letter must be sent to each rights holder, generally by email. Often, the client provides a model letter. If not, the freelancer should compose a form letter and get the client's approval before it goes out.

A good permission request letter is precise and concise in the way it presents the information and specifies the rights requested. It should list the full bibliographic citation of the material to be used, including author, title of work, date, page number(s), and word count. If possible, the request letter should include the copyright line as published in the original, and should include all details of the proposed use, such as author of the forthcoming book, title, publisher, publication date, price, territory of planned distribution, page length, and print run. The letter should include a detailed description of all rights the publisher is seeking, both print and electronic. Some rights holders also require the ISBN of the publication from which the quoted material is taken.

Many request letters contain a release form that, when signed by the copyright holder, constitutes a contract in lieu of any other document. Most major publishers ignore the release and send back a contract of their own, but a built-in release increases the chance of timely responses from individuals and small organizations. A sample permission request letter is shown in Appendix B at the end of this book.

Some rights holders require that each request include a copy of the manuscript page(s) containing the quoted material, and it is usually helpful to include this even if it is not required, because it allows the rights holder to (a) verify that it really is material that they control, and (b) see the context in which their material will be used. When placing the request electronically, the manuscript pages can often be submitted as PDF attachments or as screenshots embedded in the body of an email.

The first round of requests is only the beginning. Predictably, some rights holders will fail to respond, and others will respond by referring the requestor to one or more other parties. Another factor is location. When

Copyright and Permissions

the client is seeking rights beyond the United States, it is very likely that different rights holders will control a given item for different territories: one for Canada, another for the UK, and so on. This is the phase of the project when the permissions editor needs to be resourceful and persistent in tracking down rights holders and following up with those who have not responded within a reasonable time. Turnaround times vary greatly. Some rights holders will reply within a few days, whereas others may take four to six weeks. The permissions departments of some large publishers routinely work with a backlog of eight weeks or more.

Step 4: Preparing Acknowledgments

Once permissions have been cleared, the permissions editor is usually responsible for submitting an acknowledgments manuscript to the client. This is a list of the permission items that the client will include in the acknowledgments section of the publication. Acknowledgments generally include three elements:

1. identification of the permission item,
2. a copyright notice, and
3. a courtesy phrase such as "used by permission."

Recall from the section "How Is Copyright Established?" that a copyright notice consists of the word *copyright* or the symbol ©, the date of creation or publication, and the name of the copyright owner.

Clients may prefer or require a given style for acknowledgments; for example, if the publication is a sociology textbook, acknowledgments should follow American Sociological Association style. Acknowledgments are usually listed in order of appearance in the manuscript, but some publishers may prefer another organizational system. Several examples of acknowledgments are shown in Appendix A at the end of this book.

Compiling the acknowledgments manuscript can be a breeze if the permissions editor has populated the permissions database, especially the "Credit" field, with all the information the client will want to include in the acknowledgment. This is best done while the project is in progress, starting with the first items that are granted. For this reason, it is important to ask the client for acknowledgment style guidelines early in the project.

The accuracy required in writing an acknowledgments manuscript is comparable to that necessary in preparing an index or a library catalog: if an acknowledgment contains an error, it is worse than useless; it can actually be the source of misinformation for others who will rely on it. More important, a proper acknowledgment is almost always a condition of permission. By failing to supply an acknowledgment, or by supplying an erroneous one, the permissions editor could leave the publisher vulnerable to a penalty fee or even charges of infringement.

Some rights holders require that their acknowledgment appear adjacent to the quoted material, rather than in the front or back matter. There may also be other requirements, such as the rights holder's wish to approve the final layout or the context in which their material appears. The permissions editor should notify the client immediately of any such special requirements. If the client is unable or unwilling to accommodate the copyright holder, the permissions editor may be asked to negotiate a mutually acceptable solution.

Negotiating Fees

Some rights holders are so pleased to see their work reproduced that they will grant permission gratis, or in exchange for a copy of the publication. Most permissions, however, carry a fee. Fees vary almost infinitely according to the scope of the proposed use, the fame of the author, the age of the quoted work, and, some would say, the greed of the rights holder.

Clients typically assign each permissions project a budget based on how much the permissions cost for comparable projects in the past, or for the previous edition of the book now being revised. However, especially with first editions, the budget the client has in mind may not be realistic, given the number and complexity of permission items in the project. Another factor that can greatly increase permission costs is the addition of many electronic formats to a project that was formerly print, or a simple combination of print-plus-CD. An experienced permissions editor can sometimes prevent headaches by identifying "budget busters" at the beginning of a project, giving the client a chance to scale back the

Copyright and Permissions

number or complexity of permission items, or to avoid a troublesome rights holder. The more realistic the budget, the better the chances of successful negotiation for any fees that are out of line.

When negotiating with a rights holder who has requested an unacceptably high fee, the permissions editor should serve as an intermediary between the client and the rights holder, not only conveying each side's position to the other, but also remaining aware of whether both parties are basing their arguments on defensible provisions of copyright law. Of course, it is the client who is paying for the permissions editor's services, but the permissions editor also has a professional reputation to uphold. To avoid being caught in the middle of a legal dispute, the permissions editor should make it clear to all parties that it is the client who makes all final decisions about what is used and in what context.

One negotiating strategy that is very common in the entertainment field, and can be used to the publisher's advantage, is "most favored nations," an arrangement whereby a copyright holder is assured that no other party granting permission for a comparable use will receive a higher fee than the copyright holder does. If, for example, a prospective publisher offers $500 per work on a most favored nations basis, each copyright holder knows that no one else will be paid more than $500. But if one copyright holder insists on $750, then *all* those participating in the project will receive $750.

The most favored nations arrangement (or "favored nations," as it is sometimes called) can, however, also work to the publisher's disadvantage. If permissions were sought with the fee question left open, and one copyright holder specified $500 most favored nations, this would mean that a subsequent permission priced at $2,000 would require also paying $2,000 to the party who specified most favored nations. According to some authorities, copyright holders who did *not* request most favored nations would *also* need to be paid $2,000, or at least be notified that this amount is being paid and offered the opportunity to accept or waive an equal fee.

It occasionally happens that the parties cannot come to an agreement, and permission is not granted. In such cases, the client will need to delete the disputed material. The permissions editor should notify the copyright holder in a letter or email that, regrettably, the material will not appear in the prospective publication.

Dead Ends, Denials, and Disclaimers

Sometimes permission cannot be secured because it is not possible to contact the rights holder. In other cases, the rights holder may have died, leaving an estate that is in dispute. Sometimes it is not even possible to determine who the rights holder is for a permission item. You may recall the example of clouds and wikis in Part II.

In other cases, permission is denied. An experienced permissions editor may be able to warn the publisher of likely denials, for example, in the case of material that is being used in a derogatory context. Seeking permission to use material that is paraphrased, adapted, or otherwise modified can also result in a denial because the rights holder wants to retain control over exactly how the material is presented.

The first thing a permissions editor should do upon receiving a denial is to notify the client. Next, it is usually worthwhile to go back to the rights holder and attempt to address whatever concerns the denial is based upon. Occasionally the cause is a simple misunderstanding. For example, a rights holder may assume that no fee will be paid because the request letter did not offer a fee. As another example, a rights holder may not understand the meaning of *nonexclusive* when the request letter asks for nonexclusive permission. What it means is that the rights holder will retain all rights not specified in the request; the requestor is not seeking to become the exclusive user of the material.

In other cases, the rights holder understands the request perfectly well, but may be unwilling to grant all the rights that are requested in the form letter. When this happens, the client may be willing to scale back the provisions of the contract to accommodate the rights holder's restrictions. It is important to note, however, that a freelancer does not have the authority to make such changes without the client's approval.

When a rights holder denies permission and gives one or more concrete reasons for the decision, the permissions editor should make every effort to convey the exact wording of the reasons to the client. For example, if the copyright holder divulges the rationale in a phone conversation and is unwilling to confirm it in writing, the permissions editor should convey this in an email to the client. This may help the client to avert future denials by modifying the proposed use or by avoiding the use of works by a troublesome copyright holder.

Although denials are, of course, frustrating, they also provide an opportunity for the permissions editor to shine. By the time a permission is denied, a book or other project is often at the stage where simply deleting the denied content would leave a gaping hole. To fill the hole, someone needs to provide a rewrite or a visual, and clients are often greatly relieved if a knowledgeable and resourceful permissions editor can take the lead in providing this. When creating content to replace a piece of denied copyrighted material, be aware that the denial potentially subjects the replacement to a high level of scrutiny; the replacement must not be a "copycat" version of the denied material. Here are some further tips.

- A rewrite must be in one's own words; it would be a violation of copyright to "patch write" using words, phrases, and sentence structure from the original.
- A photograph cannot be replaced with a drawing of the same visual content that exists in the photo; such a drawing would be derivative work, and derivatives are protected by copyright just as the original is.
- Data can generally be used without permission as long as proper attribution is made, so if permission is refused for a data graph, it may be possible to write a paragraph summarizing the data that would have been displayed in the graph.

The key principle to keep in mind is that copyright protects not ideas, but rather the tangible expression of ideas. By creating a suggested replacement that conveys the ideas or concepts embodied in the denied material, a permissions editor can be a hero and prevent the permission denial from derailing the project.

For some clients, when a permission is denied, there is a temptation to go ahead and use the material with a disclaimer such as "Every effort has been made to contact the copyright holder of [a given selection], and the publisher would appreciate communication from anyone knowing the whereabouts of the party who has the authority to grant permission." Although such a notice may help establish goodwill in the event that a copyright holder comes forward, it does not legally protect the client against charges of infringement.

For this reason, a freelance permissions editor should never advise a client to go ahead with the use of copyrighted material whose owner cannot be located, much less with material for which permission was denied. If the client intends to use the uncleared material with a disclaimer, the freelancer would be well advised to write a personal disclaimer to go on record with the client, confirming that the client assumes any risks of possible infringement.

Freelancers should also protect themselves by ensuring that the client is responsible for paying all agreed-upon permission fees. It never hurts to use phrases like "On behalf of X Publisher, I request …" and "X Publisher has confirmed that the fee you have requested is acceptable" to remind rights holders that the client is the one making use of the material, and it is the client, not the permissions editor, who enters into the contract with the rights holders.

I once worked on a project where the author was responsible for paying all the permission fees but he didn't do so. Rights holders kept coming after me for at least a year! I had to complain to the publisher several times; they kept saying they didn't know what the problem was, but finally the truth came out.

This concludes the discussion of how to accomplish a permissions project. If you've enjoyed learning how the process works, you may want to build permissions editing into your career plans.

Tips for Finding Permissions Editing Jobs

The first step in becoming a successful permissions editor is to start small. Taking on a large, complex project before you are ready would be like trying to play a Bach violin concerto after studying violin for a couple of weeks. It will be much wiser to gain experience in small increments.

If you are already working as an editorial freelancer, seek out a fellow freelancer who specializes in permissions and ask about opportunities to help with a portion of a project, or to subcontract a small project under the experienced freelancer's supervision. If you decide to approach prospective clients directly, be honest with them about your beginner status.

Permissions editing is generally done on a freelance basis, but there are also many in-house jobs that deal with copyright, permissions, and rights clearance in one way or another. These jobs are found not only in publishing companies and literary agencies but also in law firms that specialize in intellectual property, public libraries and university libraries, museums, and rights clearance organizations like Art Resource, the Authors Registry, Broadcast Music, Inc. (BMI), and Copyright Clearance Center. These in-house jobs can be an excellent way to learn the business before going freelance. The greatest demand for freelance permissions editors is with clients who produce publications incorporating large amounts of preexisting material. These include:

- college textbook publishers
- publishers of anthologies
- publishers of scholarly and professional books and journals
- music publishers
- advertising agencies
- freelance design studios
- corporate public relations departments
- video and electronic production companies
- multimedia producers
- web designers

In approaching clients outside of the publishing industry, describing oneself as a "copyright specialist" or "rights clearance consultant" may be more effective than "permissions editor" in paving the way to the appropriate department.

Within college textbook publishing, some of the larger publishers have a centralized permissions department; an advanced search of LinkedIn with the keyword *permissions* brings up several results of this kind. Many other publishers have a manager of editorial services whose job it is to find and hire qualified freelancers; this can also be a good place to start. A more specialized approach is to contact acquisitions or development editors, or both, in a given academic discipline where the applicant has solid expertise.

Permissions editing may be fascinating and enjoyable work, but the freelancer needs to know how well it is going to pay. Depending on the client, payment may be offered by the hour, by the permission item, or by the job. Because the permissions editor has no control over how difficult it will be to contact a given rights holder, accepting payment by the item or by the job is more of a gamble in this field than in, say, writing or copyediting. Conversely, clients may see payment by the hour as a gamble from their own point of view. Often both sides can be satisfied with hourly pay when a certain number of hours or a sum is agreed on as a target at the outset of the project.

As in many other kinds of freelancing, success as a permissions editor depends on such qualities as reliability, precision, thoroughness, and efficiency. A job accomplished on time, on budget, and with cheerful professionalism is the best way to generate new assignments from a satisfied client and build a favorable reputation with the client's colleagues.

References

Creative Commons. *Mission: What Is Creative Commons?* Available at creativecommons.org/.

Facebook. *Terms: Statement of Rights and Responsibilities.* Revised 2011. Facebook © 2012. Web. facebook.com/legal/terms?ref=pf.

Hamblett, Mark. "Chin Decides Google Books Settlement Would 'Go Too Far.'" *New York Law Journal,* March 23, 2011. Web. tinyurl.com/7lzfujg or newyorklawjournal.com/PubArticleNY.jsp?id=1202487454956&slreturn=1.

Harris, Sidney. Cartoon. Copyright © 1993 by Sidney Harris, ScienceCartoonsPlus.com . Used by permission.

Hasbrouck, Edward. "Publishers Sue the Internet Archive for Scanning Books." National Writers Union, June 1, 2020. Web. https://nwu.org/publishers-sue-the-internet-archive-for-scanning-books/

Internet Archive. *Internet Archive's Terms of Use, Privacy Policy, and Copyright Policy.* December 31, 2014. https://archive.org/about/terms.php

Kimball, Whitney. "The Internet Archive Fights Wiki Citation Wars With Books." Gizmodo, November 4, 2019. Web. https://gizmodo.com/the-internet-archive-fights-wiki-citation-wars-with-boo-1839609540

Stempel, Jonathan. "Google Defeats Authors in U.S. Book-Scanning Lawsuit." Reuters Technology News, November 14, 2013. Web. reuters.com/article/us-google-books-idUSBRE9AD0TT20131114.

Twitter. *Terms of Service: Your Rights; Twitter Rights.* Revised 2012. © 2012 Twitter. Web. twitter.com/tos.

United States Copyright Office. *Copyright Basics.* Washington, DC: US Government Printing Office, reviewed 2012. Web. copyright.gov/circs/circ01.pdf.

United States Copyright Office. *Fair Use.* Washington, DC: US Government Printing Office, reviewed 2009. Web. copyright.gov/fls/fl102.html.

APPENDIX A:
SAMPLE ACKNOWLEDGMENTS

Literature: T. S. Eliot, "Little Gidding" from *Four Quartets* and *Collected Poems, 1909–1962.* Copyright © 1943 by T. S. Eliot and renewed 1971 by Esmé Valerie Eliot. Reprinted by permission of Harcourt Brace Jovanovich, Inc., and Faber & Faber, Ltd.

Science (Medicine): Vaughan Sarrazin MS, Rosenthal GE. Finding pure and simple truths with administrative data. *JAMA.* 2012; 307(13):1433–1435. doi:10.1001/jama.2012.404 . © 2012 American Medical Association. All Rights Reserved. Used by permission.

Science (Psychology): Schumpe, B. M., Bélanger, J. J., Moyano, M., & Nisa, C. F. (2020). The role of sensation seeking in political violence: An extension of the Significance Quest Theory. *Journal of Personality and Social Psychology, 118*(4), 743–761. doi.org/10.1037/pspp0000223. Copyright © 2020, American Psychological Association. Used by permission.

Social Science (Sociology): Abelson, Reed, and Michael Barbaro. 2006. "Law Aimed at Wal-Mart May Be Hard to Replicate." *New York Times*, January 16: pp. C1, C2. Copyright © 2006 by The New York Times Company. Reprinted by permission.

ELSA PETERSON

Music: Béla Bartók, *Mikrokosmos No. 125,* "Boating." © Copyright 1940 by Hawkes and Son (London) Ltd. Copyright renewed. Reprinted by permission of Boosey & Hawkes, Inc.

Cartoon: © The New Yorker Collection 2012 Emily Flake from cartoonbank.com. All Rights Reserved.

APPENDIX B:
SAMPLE PERMISSION REQUEST LETTER

[Letterhead of prospective user or of permissions editor]

Date _____

Company
Attn. Permissions Manager
Street
City, State, Zip

Dear [Rights holder]:

On behalf of XX Publisher, I request permission to use the following material:

> Excerpt (identified by title and/or page numbers)
>
> From (author, title, publication date, copyright notice)
>
> [any other relevant and available information]

This material will appear in the forthcoming [nth] edition of a college textbook entitled Title, compiled by Author and Author, which will be published by XX Publishers in January [year] and sold for an anticipated price of $xx. A print run of x,000 units is planned for the life of the edition.

ELSA PETERSON

We request nonexclusive permission including print and electronic world rights in English for this and all future editions, supplements, and alternate versions of our book. This permission will in no way restrict your right to license the material to others, or to use it in any other way.

You may grant permission by signing below and returning one copy of this letter to me. Unless otherwise specified, acknowledgment will be given to author, publisher, and copyright holder as shown above. In the event that you do not control the rights to this material, I would appreciate a referral to the proper party.

Sincerely,
[signed]
Freelance Permissions Editor
On behalf of XX Publisher

Permission is hereby granted to XX Publisher for use of the above as specified.

Signature _____

Name (printed) _____

Date _____

Address _____

Fee _____

Tax ID _____

Phone _____

APPENDIX C:
RECOMMENDED RESOURCES

Library of Congress, Copyright Office, 101 Independence Avenue, S.E., Washington, DC 20559-6000, telephone (202) 707-3000, copyright.gov. *Copyright Basics* and many other informational circulars on copyright topics are available at copyright.gov/circs/. To search for a copyright registration or renewal, go to copyright.gov/records/. For more entertaining (but no less accurate) information on copyright, visit copyright.gov and click on "Taking the Mystery out of Copyright (for Students and Teachers)."

Association of American Publishers, 50 F Street NW, Washington, DC 20001-1530, phone (202) 347-3375 / fax (202) 347-3690, publishers.org/.

An Author's Guide to Fighting Internet Copyright Infringements: How Publishers and Website Owners Can Protect Intellectual Property Online. Morris Rosenthal. Foner Books, 2012.

Authors Guild v. Google Settlement Resources Page at tinyurl.com/62679v or authorsguild.org/advocacy/articles/settlement-resources.html.

Authors Registry, 31 East 32nd Street, 7th Floor, New York, NY 10016, phone (212) 563-6920 / fax (212) 564-5363. Can also be found at: authorsregistry.org; email staff@authorsregistry.org.

Center for Internet and Society, Stanford Law School cyberlaw.stanford.edu/focus-areas/copyright-and-fair-use.

Copyright Office: Celebrating World Intellectual Property Day copyright.gov/docs/wipo2011.html.

Copyright Website LLC. benedict.com/Digital/Internet/DMCA/DMCA.aspx/.

Creative Commons: creativecommons.org/.

Creative Commons (2019). *Creative Commons for Educators and Librarians*. Available for download and in print from creativecommons.org/2019/12/06/cc-for-educators-and-librarians-is-available.

Digital Copyright: Protecting Intellectual Property on the Internet. Jessica Litman. Prometheus Books, 2001; paperback edition 2006.

Educause: educause.edu/Resources/Browse/Copyright/17092.

Electronic Frontier Foundation: eff.org/; eff.org/issues/dmca.

Intellectual Property and the National Information Infrastructure: The Report of the Working Group on Intellectual Property Rights. Bruce A. Lehman, Asst. Secretary of Commerce and Commissioner of Patents and Trademarks; Chair, Information Infrastructure Task Force. Washington, DC: United States Patent and Trademark Office, 1995. Available online at uspto.gov/web/offices/com/doc/ipnii/.

Patent, Copyright & Trademark: An Intellectual Property Desk Reference. Richard Stim, Nolo Press, 2009.

Tales from the Public Domain: Bound by Law? Keith Aoki, James Boyle, and Jennifer Jenkins. Duke Center for the Study of the Public Domain. Copyright © 2006 Keith Aoki, James Boyle, Jennifer Jenkins. Available online at web.law.duke.edu/cspd/comics/?goback=.gde_3870454_member_162322546.

INDEX

© (copyright symbol), 8–9

acknowledgments
   preparing, 43–44
   samples, 53–54
advertising, on social media and websites, 23
anti-copyright notices, 29
Association of American Publishers (AAP), 26
authors
   copyright assigned to publishers by, 7
   examination of manuscripts by, 35–37
   in Google suit, 26
   multiple, 23–25
   permissions editors hired by, 34
Authors Guild, 26

Berne Convention, 11
Bono, Sonny, 16
book reviews, 13

Canada, 18
Chin, Denny, 26
Clinton, Bill, 16
Constitution (US)
   copyright under, 3, 27
   First Amendment of, 13
controlled digital lending, 26
copyleft, 29
copyright, 1–4
   Creative Commons and, 27–29
   Digital Millennium Copyright Act on, 20
   duration of, 16–18, 30–31
   establishing (registering), 7–11
   facts and fallacies on, 4–7
   fair use versus, 13–15
   material not covered by, 11–12
   permissions editing to obtain use of, 33–34
   public domain versus, 12–15
Copyright Act (1909), 7–8
Copyright Act (1976), 7–8, 16
Copyright Basics, 3–4, 12
Copyright Clearance Center (CCC), 41–42

copyright holders
   acknowledging, 43–44
   contacting, 40–43
   denials of permission by, 46–48
   fees paid to, 44–46
   in permissions database, 39–40
copyright notices, 5, 8–9
   anti-copyright notices and, 29
Copyright Office Form CO, 10
Copyright Records Reading Room (Library of Congress), 17
Copyright Registration, 11
© (copyright symbol), 8–9
Copyright Term Extension Act (Sonny Bono Copyright Term Extension Act; SBCTEA; 1998), 16–17, 30
copywriting, 4
Creative Commons, 27–29

data, rights to, 47
database for permissions editing, 37–40
dead ends, 46
denials of permission, 46–48
derivative works, 47
digital collaboration, 23–25
Digital Millennium Copyright Act (DMCA; 1998), 20
   on online service providers, 21
duration of copyright, 16–18, 30–31
Duration of Copyright, 16–17

Electronic Copyright Office (eCO), of the Library of Congress, 10

Facebook, 22–23
fair dealing, 14–15
fair use, 13–15
   misconceptions on, 5
   permissions not needed for use of, 36, 37
Fair Use Index, 13
favored nations arrangements, 45
fees
   negotiating, 44–46
   responsibilities for, 48
freelance permissions editing, 49

Google, books digitized by, 25–27
government publications, 12

ideas, copyright on, 4, 11–12
in-house permissions editing positions, 49
international agreements on copyright, 11, 18
internet
   contacting rights holders using, 41–42
   Digital Millennium Copyright Act on, 20
   social media on, 20–23
   Terms of Use for material on, 6
   use of material published on, 5
Internet Archive (IA), 26–27

libel, 15–16
Library of Congress
　Copyright Office of, 3
　Copyright Records Reading
　　Room of, 17
　Electronic Copyright
　　Office of, 10
　registering copyright
　　with, 6–10
LinkedIn, 49
location of rights holders, 42–43

manuscripts, permissions
　editing of, 35–37
Mexico, 18
Mickey Mouse Protection Act. *See*
　Sonny Bono Copyright Term
　Extension Act
most favored nations
　arrangements, 45

orphan works, 25–26

Patent and Trademark
　Office, US, 15
patents, 15–16
permission request letters, 42
　sample, 55–56
permissions editing, 33–34
　acknowledgments
　　prepared in, 43–44
　building database for, 37–40
　contacting copyright
　　holders in, 40–43

　dead ends and
　　denials in, 46–48
　finding jobs in, 48–50
　manuscript
　　examination in, 35–37
　negotiating fees in, 44–45
photographs, 22–23
　drawings derivative of, 47
　permissions for, 34
plagiarism, of material from
　internet, 5
privacy, 15–16
public domain, 12–15
　copyright on material from, 6
　nonrenewed copyrighted
　　material in, 17
　permissions not needed for
　　use of, 36–37
publishers
　copyright transferred to, 7
　definition of, 3
　in-house permissions editing
　　positions in, 49
　obtaining permissions
　　from, 40–41

registration of copyright, 8–10
　fallacies on, 6
release forms, 42
renewals of copyrights, 17

service marks, 15
ShareAlike license, 29
slogans, 4–5

social media, 20–23
    Terms of Use for, 6
Sonny Bono Copyright Term Extension Act (SBCTEA; US), 16–17, 30
Stanford Copyright Renewal Database, 17

Terms of Use, 6, 21
    for Facebook, 22–23
    for Internet Archive, 26
    for Twitter, 24–25
textbook publishing, 49
trademarks, 5, 15–16
transfer of copyright, 7
transformative use, 14
Twitter, 24–25

United States
    government publications of, 12
    international copyright agreements of, 11
Universal Copyright Convention, 11

viral licensing (copyleft), 29

Walt Disney Company, 30, 31
websites
    contacting rights holders using, 40–41
    Terms of Use for material on, 6
    use of material published on, 5
wikis (collaborative works), 24
work for hire agreements, 8

About the Author

Elsa Peterson began working with intellectual property in the early 1980s when she was copyright administrator for European American Music Distributors Corporation. Her most recent in-house position was as a Senior Developmental Editor for Psychology with McGraw-Hill Higher Education. She has more than thirty years of experience as a freelance permissions editor, picture researcher, and developmental editor. Additionally, she has taught classes in copyright for Greenwich (CT) Continuing Education and the Editorial Freelancers Association's education program, and has presented talks on copyright and permissions through the Text and Academic Authors Association. Elsa holds a BA with highest honors in music from the University of California at Riverside and an MA in music history from Case Western Reserve University.

About the
Editorial Freelancers Association (EFA)

Celebrating 50 Years!
Dedicated to the Education and Growth
of Editorial Freelancers

The EFA is a national not-for-profit — 501(c)6 — organization, headquartered in New York City, run by member volunteers, all of whom are also freelancers. The EFA's members, experienced in a wide range of professional skills, live and work all across the United States and in other countries.

A pioneer in organizing freelancers into a network for mutual support and advancement, the EFA is now recognized throughout the publishing industry as the source for professional editorial assistance.

We welcome people of every race, color, culture, religion or no religion, gender identity, gender expression, age, national or ethnic origin, ancestry, citizenship, education, ability, health, neurotype, marital/parental status, socio-economic background, sexual orientation, and/or military status. We are nothing without our members, and encourage everyone to volunteer and to participate in our community.

The EFA sells a variety of specialized booklets, not unlike this one, on topics of interest to editorial freelancers at the-efa.org.

The EFA hosts online, asynchronous courses, real-time webinars, and on-demand recorded webinars designed especially for freelance editors, writers, and other editorial specialists around the world. You can learn more about our Education Program at the-efa.org.

To learn about these and other EFA offerings, visit the-efa.org and join us on social media:

Twitter: @EFAFreelancers
Instagram: @efa_editors
Facebook: editorialfreelancersassociation
LinkedIn: editorial-freelancers